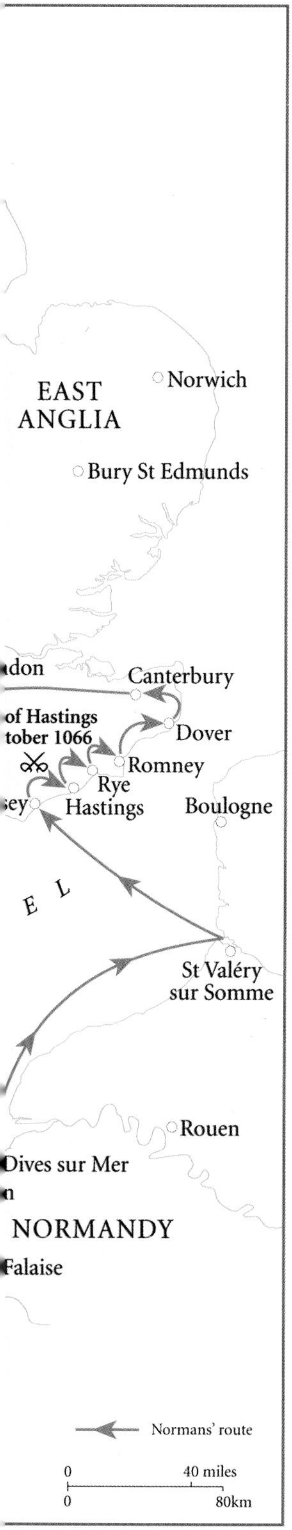

FOREWORD

Map labels (left):

EAST ANGLIA

Norwich

Bury St Edmunds

don Canterbury

of Hastings
tober 1066 Dover

Romney

Rye

Hastings Boulogne

E L

St Valéry
sur Somme

Rouen

Dives sur Mer

NORMANDY

Falaise

Normans' route

0 40 miles
0 80km

THE BAYEUX TAPESTRY is f⁓ ⁓sociated with William the Conqueror, ⁓ ⁓e Battle of Hastings. And ye⁓ studied, it keeps some ⁓ came to the attenti⁓ 17th century, it '⁓ ⁓tant speculation. I⁓ ⁓ations, television docun⁓ ⁓ces and seminars in many ⁓ ⁓s images feature in thousands of books, ⁓ publicity material and souvenirs of all kinds.

The Tapestry is usually presented as a visual justification for the conquest of England by William, Duke of Normandy. Its history is also bound up with that of the town of Bayeux itself, which claims it for its own: but there the common ground stops. Everything else is the subject of debate. Every so often, historians and textile experts stir up debates, and newspapers seize upon the issues. The big questions – which will doubtless never have an answer – are, who had it made, and where. Queen Matilda has long since been set aside as the patron of the work, while the role of Bishop Odo has recently been questioned in favour of Queen Edith or Count Eustace of Boulogne. Most authorities maintain that the tapestry must have been created in Canterbury, but other candidates include Normandy and the Val de Loire (Saint Florent de Saumur). And what are we to make of the minor characters such as Aelfgyva, Turold, Wadard or Vital? Despite the many interpretations put forward, they remain an enigma to us.

The authors of this guide have a thorough knowledge of the latest thinking about the Tapestry. But they go beyond a mere inventory of its secrets and describe with evident delight the history it relates. To meet the challenge of saying everything – or nearly everything – that there is to say in a short guide is no mean achievement, and they have succeeded brilliantly.

ABOVE: *William the Conqueror, first Norman king of England, on a silver penny. His victory in 1066 changed English history.*

Sylvette Lemagnen
Curator
Bayeux Tapestry Museum
and Media Centre

RIGHT: *The Bayeux Tapestry as visitors see it: a vibrant picture-strip memorial of one of European history's most celebrated episodes.*

WHO MADE THE TAPESTRY?

The Bayeux Tapestry was almost certainly made in the 1070s and probably for Bishop Odo, Earl of Kent, William the Conqueror's half-brother. It could have been hung in this warrior-bishop's great hall, either in England or Normandy, but it was quite possibly unveiled publicly to mark the consecration in 1077 of the rebuilt Cathedral of Notre Dame in Bayeux. Curiously, the chronicler Wace (born *c.*1100) does not mention the Tapestry, though he lived nearby – the cathedral priests probably kept it locked up.

The Tapestry is listed in an inventory of cathedral possessions in 1476. Whether it had been there for the previous four centuries no one is certain. It was traditionally known as Queen Matilda's Tapestry (Matilda of Flanders was the Conqueror's wife), but there is no evidence of any connection with her.

The style of embroidery suggests that the fingers plying the needles and thread were English. Details of scenes are stylistically similar to decorations in Anglo-Saxon manuscripts, and in the Latin text some names are spelled in the English way. It was possibly created in Canterbury, where there was, at

RIGHT: *Tree devices such as this one, in swirling Anglo-Saxon style, pop up throughout the Tapestry, sometimes to frame scenes, sometimes as part of the action. Here a Norman lookout keeps watch from the branches.*

the time, a famous school of decorative embroidery.

The design could be the work of one artist, perhaps a man with personal knowledge of military equipment and ships. The use of the same colours on unconnected areas suggests that the embroiderers were following a traced outline or cartoon, prepared by the designer. Similar wall hangings are known, including

BELOW: *The decorations include many animals, often fantastic creations, and puzzling human figures. Later, in the Battle of Hastings scenes, these are replaced by severed heads and limbs, and stripped corpses.*

The Tapisserie

The strip of cloth at which thousands of visitors to Bayeux gaze every year is not a tapestry at all, but an embroidery. The picture-strip story is stitched, not woven – each scene and character worked by needle and thread onto a long strip of cloth, fastened to a backing material. The words *tapis* and *tapisserie* were used in the Middle Ages to describe any hanging textile decoration, floor covering or furniture throw, and the Bayeux Tapestry it will no doubt remain.

Viking examples from ship burials, but none like the Bayeux Tapestry in scale or preservation. Repaired over the years, and now carefully conserved in its Bayeux museum, it tells the story of the events that led up to William's victory over Harold at Hastings. A decorative border above and below the action is filled with around 500 smaller figures, mostly animals, but also occasional and often baffling humans. The last section is missing, but otherwise the Tapestry has survived in miraculously good condition, its colours still bright, and its contents a perennial source of interest to historians and public alike.

ABOVE: '*... a very long and very narrow strip of linen, embroidered with figures and inscriptions representing the Conquest of England.*' This is how the clerks at Bayeux Cathedral describe the Tapestry in the inventory of 1476. *Battle scenes depict vividly the mayhem of medieval combat.*

Facts and figures

The Tapestry is 68.38 metres (224 feet) long and 50cm (20 inches) wide. It is made of nine (some sources say eight) bands of linen, sewn together. The thread is two-ply wool yarn, with some linen thread, the stitching mostly stem stitch and laid-and-couched. There are at least ten plant-dye colours. Appearing in 58 episodic scenes are 626 characters, 174 horses, 55 dogs, 37 ships, 49 trees and 37 buildings. Shown here is a yawning Norman in William's castle.

THE TALE UNFOLDED

The Tapestry story starts in 1064. Edward the Confessor bids farewell to Harold, off on a mission to Normandy. Blown off course, Harold lands in the wrong place and is held hostage by Count Guy of Ponthieu, before being released on the orders of Guy's neighbour, Duke William of Normandy – not a man to be trifled with. Harold therefore helps William fight another neighbour, Duke Conan of Brittany. As a reward, he is knighted by William and also swears some kind of oath, before returning home.

Within hours of Edward's death, in January 1066, Harold is king. Spies tell William, who orders war preparations to back his own claim to the English throne. The Tapestry

ABOVE: *How it begins. King Edward the Confessor, still hale if not hearty, sends Harold off to Normandy. Was Harold's mission to tell William that the crown was his?*

ABOVE: *A grotesque carved face grins from a column in Holy Trinity Church, Bosham, Sussex. Then a major seaport, this was where Harold had his hall.*

now ignores Harold's brief reign, and his successful repelling of the first challenge to his rule, from Harald Hardrada of Norway, at Stamford Bridge, Yorkshire, in September. Instead, it shows the Normans building ships and collecting men, horses and stores for their invasion. William crosses the Channel, landing his army near Pevensey in Sussex. The invaders build fortifications, forage for food and loot the countryside. Meanwhile, unseen in the Tapestry account, the English king is hurrying south to confront them.

LEFT: *Harold and his party dine in his great hall at Bosham. They sit in an upper room, or perhaps in a gallery, reached by a staircase. The border below contains an enigmatic allusion to Aesop's Fables. A vain crow opens its beak to sing, and so drops its food into the mouth of the fox (though the fox looks more like a lynx or leopard). Like the crow, is Harold to be the victim of flattery and pride?*

The Tapestry shows the Battle of Hastings of 14 October in violent detail, and chiefly from the viewpoint of the Norman cavalry. The deaths of Harold, and his two brothers Gurth and Leofwine, break English resistance, and the Tapestry tale ends with the Normans pursuing the remnants of the English army.

So ended 500 years of Saxon rule in England. In December 1066 William I was crowned in Westminster Abbey. The Conqueror swiftly crushed any resistance, laid waste the North, bullied the Scots into submission and ordered the Domesday Book to document his Conquest. He visited England rarely, leaving the realm largely in the control of Odo, as Norman barons seized the lands of dead or dispossessed English nobles. By the time the Tapestry was revealed to the world, the conquest was complete and the course of British history had been changed forever.

ABOVE: *William, Duke of Normandy, listens to a messenger. His bearing (and his haircut) are warlike. He and Harold are, in different ways, both heroes of the story.*

History in the making

The Anglo-Saxon Chronicle records the tumultuous events of 1066, from the death of King Edward after which 'Harold the earl succeeded to the kingdom and held it forty weeks and one day'. It describes how 'William the earl landed at Hastings on St Michael's Day, and Harold came from the north, and fought against him before all his army had come up; and there he fell, and his two brothers Gurth and Leofwine, and William subdued this land'.

LEADING CHARACTERS IN THE TAPESTRY

Edward the Confessor (born 1004) became ruler of England in 1042. The son of Aethelred II (the Unready; 978–1016), he had spent much of his life in exile in Normandy, and his reign saw a growth of Norman influence in the English Church and in land holding. A pious builder of churches (hence his title), Edward struggled against the wiles of England's most

BELOW: *William's statue in his home town of Falaise. He claimed that in 1051 the childless (and that year Godwin-less) King Edward promised him the English crown.* The Anglo-Saxon Chronicle *says William came to England that year 'with a great band of Frenchmen', but mystery shrouds this visit.*

unscrupulous political operator, Earl Godwin. Godwin contrived a marriage between Edward and his daughter Edith, but the king failed (or refused) to sire a son.

Harold (born *c*.1020) was Godwin's second son, more popular than his disreputable older brother Sweyn, and heir to his father's political legacy. Exiled by Edward in 1051, the Godwin clan returned in force the next year. By kicking out Edward's Norman archbishop, Robert of Jumièges, they alienated the papacy. Nor were they universally loved by the English earls. Even so, after Godwin died in 1053, the soldierly Harold Godwinson became the chief man of the kingdom.

Successors from afar

Edward had restored the Wessex royal line in England (after the Dane Cnut, 1016–35, and Cnut's two sons). But he had no son and heir. The most legitimate successors to the Confessor landed in England in 1057. They were Edward the Exile, son of Edmund II Ironside (briefly king in 1016), and his son Edgar the Aetheling. Edward had lived in Hungary as an exile, but now returned, only to die, mysteriously, soon after reaching England. With Edgar still a teenager, Harold was left in pole position in the race for the crown.

LEFT: *Here the Tapestry shows Eustace, Count of Boulogne, recognizable by his un-Norman moustache. At a critical moment in the Battle of Hastings, Eustace points towards William, as the Conqueror raises his helmet to show his fellow Normans he is still alive.*

ABOVE: *William and his two half-brothers. Odo, the battling Bishop of Bayeux, is on his right, Robert of Mortain on his left. Despite his unpleasant disposition, as a man of God, Odo was forbidden to shed blood, so at Hastings he bore a mace, rather than a sword.*

In Normandy, Duke William ruled with an iron fist. Born *c.*1027, the illegitimate son of Duke Robert I and a Falaise girl named Herleva, William was left fatherless by the age of 8. Survival of a perilous childhood led to a pugnacious manhood; he mastered Normandy and dominated neighbour states (France was not yet a united kingdom). Herleva produced two more sons: Odo, arrogant, greedy and very ambitious, became Bishop of Bayeux in 1049, while still a teenager;

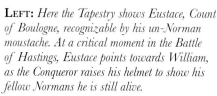

LEFT: *A portrait medal of 1060, with the rather care-worn face of Edward the Confessor.*

Robert of Mortain was more genial, perhaps even slow-witted, but loyal to his half-brother William.

A French ruler who appears, fleetingly but perhaps tellingly, in the Tapestry is Eustace II, Count of Boulogne, who fought alongside William at Hastings. Married to King Edward's sister, Godgifu, he bore a grudge against the Godwins who in 1051 refused to punish the locals after Eustace had got the worst of a mass brawl in Dover.

After Hastings, apparently unhappy with his rewards, Eustace tried to seize Dover in 1067, but failed, and later made his peace with William.

LEFT: *Harold (moustached) rides with his captor, Guy of Ponthieu. The English earl was 'admired for his great stature and elegance', according to Cornelius Vitalis.*

SECRETS AND SHADOWS

The names of the Tapestry's warriors are largely unknown. Two French rulers are shown, both featuring in Harold's earlier adventures. Guy of Ponthieu was the ruler who had previously seized Harold when the Englishman landed near the River Somme by mistake. Guy's brother Hugh fought at Hastings, and may have helped kill Harold.

The second ruler, Conan of Brittany, was a potential threat at William's back. William encouraged Breton rebels to stir up trouble, and persuaded Harold to join a military expedition into Brittany to discomfort Duke Conan further. Conan died in 1065, but many Bretons fought with William at Hastings the following year.

ABOVE: *Guy of Ponthieu ponders how to make the most of Harold's unexpected arrival.*

ABOVE: *Some pictures keep their secrets over nine centuries. What did contemporaries make of this naked couple? Why is this naked man squatting beneath the Aelfgyva figure, shown on the facing page? What is the axeman up to?*

The only two Norman knights named in the Tapestry are Wadard and Vital, both probably attached to Odo's retinue. Wadard is recorded in the Domesday Book as holding six houses in Dover and manors in eight English counties, granted by Odo. Vital also ended up with English land, thanks to Odo. Some sources refer to him as Vitalis of Canterbury, a city where the knight had houses and founded a church dedicated to St Edmund the Martyr.

The five Aelfgyvas

At least five women of high rank in the 11th century had or took the name Aelfgyva (or Aelfgifu):

1 King Aethelred's second queen
2 Emma of Normandy (Aethelred's third queen, and mother of Edward the Confessor
3 Aelfgyva of Northampton, mother of Cnut's son Harold I
4 William's daughter Agatha, betrothed to Harold
5 Harold's sister, betrothed to a Norman baron.

Which, if any, is shown in the Tapestry, and why, remains a mystery.

ABOVE: *Aelfgyva and the priest. Much has been read into their poses, and his gesture, but the meaning remains hidden.*

According to the chronicler Goscelin, Vital shipped Caen limestone across the Channel to rebuild the royal palace at Westminster and St Augustine's Abbey in Canterbury.

Named in the Tapestry but otherwise little-known to history is Turold the dwarf. He holds two horses, possibly the mounts of messengers from William to Guy of Ponthieu. Domesday lists 14 Turolds; the one whom we see in the Tapestry was perhaps an entertainer, or jongleur. His presence, and the fact that his name is so prominently stitched, suggests a well-known character.

More mysterious is the 'problem picture' of a woman and a tonsured priest, who seems to be stroking her cheek. A vaguely suggestive caption translating as 'Where a certain clerk and Aelfgyfa…' has aroused much speculation. Could this be a reference to a scandal of the day? If so, who are the couple?

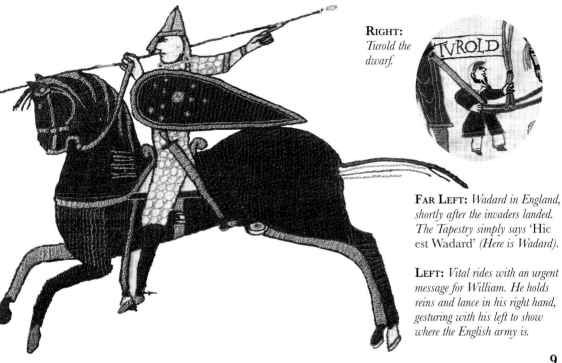

RIGHT: *Turold the dwarf.*

FAR LEFT: *Wadard in England, shortly after the invaders landed. The Tapestry simply says 'Hic est Wadard' (Here is Wadard).*

LEFT: *Vital rides with an urgent message for William. He holds reins and lance in his right hand, gesturing with his left to show where the English army is.*

9

ALLIES IN ARMS

Harold may have been sent to Normandy in 1064 to inform William about Edward's succession decision, but he may also have had a personal reason: to seek the release of his brother Wulfnoth, held hostage in Normandy since the 1050s.

Mounted and moustached, Harold looks every inch the Saxon noble. Having prayed in his own Wessex church, and enjoyed a cheerful meal, off he rides with hawk and hounds to take ship. The men wade, bare-legged, to board the vessels, which are rowed before the sails are hoisted.

Harold's ship is blown off course. The voyagers (again hitching up their clothes to splash ashore) find they are at the mouth of the Somme. The locals are not welcoming, and Harold is seized by Count Guy of Ponthieu. The Englishman maintains his cool, riding with a hawk on his wrist.

RIGHT AND ABOVE: *The 10th-century Church of Holy Trinity, Bosham, with the Tapestry picture of it. The church has a Saxon chancel arch and a Saxon tower, and kingly associations: the story goes that King Cnut's young daughter was drowned nearby, and buried here. Harold prayed at Bosham before his voyage to Normandy.*

ABOVE: *Harold wades out to his ship to begin his eventful trip across the Channel.*

As soon as William hears of Harold's misadventure, he sends two messengers at the gallop to Guy, demanding Harold's release. Harold and William meet, and the visit takes on a diplomatic tone. They talk in William's castle, probably about the hostage situation (a bearded man shown at these negotiations might be Wulfnoth), perhaps also about useful marriages (Harold to William's daughter Agatha, for one). To show his friendship, Harold agrees to help William against Conan of Brittany.

Crossing the River Couesnon, near Mont-Saint-Michel, the Normans get into difficulties in quicksands. Horses stumble,

riders fall off, soldiers carry their shields over their heads; but the English earl comes to the rescue of one comrade, carrying him to dry land on his shoulders.

The Normans attack Conan's stronghold at Dol, from which a fugitive escapes by shinning down a rope. In two subsequent actions, at Rennes and Dinan, Harold sees at first-hand the Norman cavalry, and the Normans' ruthless expertise in siege warfare. As Conan surrenders the key, on the tip of his lance, William's soldiers are enthusiastically setting fire to his castle.

BELOW: *The Normans attack Conan's castle, and a fugitive makes a hasty exit.*

LEFT: *Harold to the rescue: the earl struggles through the quagmire of Norman/French politics.*

Noble style

The Tapestry shows noblemen riding about the countryside, in a manner that changed little over centuries. The English have long hair and moustaches; the Normans have shaven necks. But their clothes and armour are very similar. The noblemen wear cloaks.

RIGHT: *Mont-Saint-Michel off the coast of Normandy. At high tide, the sea surrounds the rock. At low tide, shifting sand-banks and quicksands made it a dangerous place, before the construction of the causeway that now links it to the mainland. Parts of the abbey church date from the 11th century.*

CROWNING ISSUE

All three kings who feature in the Bayeux Tapestry are given the insignia of royalty. The text acknowledges Harold: '*Hic residet Harold rex Anglorum*' (Here sits on the throne Harold, king of the English). However, later chroniclers usually refer to Harold as a usurper; in the Domesday Book he is called 'earl' not 'king'.

Before the Brittany expedition, William looks dominant. He sits while Harold stands, apparently pleading for his brother's release. Later, William again appears at his most ducal, presenting Harold with knightly honours. The Normans claimed the oath that Harold then swore was a pledge not to oppose William as future king of England. But was it an undertaking made under duress?

The 'broken oath' gave William moral title for his invasion, alongside the charge that the English Church was corrupted by the worldly Archbishop of Canterbury, Stigand. This moral laxity won for William the invaluable support of Pope Alexander II.

RIGHT: *Harold swears on holy relics. He touches two reliquaries, containing perhaps the bones of a saint or a nail from the Cross.*

Where was Harold crowned?

Harold was crowned with rather unseemly, if understandable, haste, within a few hours of Edward's funeral. The ceremony was held either in St Paul's Cathedral or Westminster Abbey. Previous English kings had been crowned at various places, including Bath, Kingston and Winchester. If the coronation was at Westminster Abbey, it was the first in that church. William and all but one subsequent monarchs to this day followed in Harold's footsteps.

The Tapestry then shows Harold returning to England. His mood may only be guessed at. One account says that Harold came seeking William's daughter in marriage, departing amicably. Later, some English maintained that Harold was the victim of a Norman plot, though it's hard to imagine any Godwin as an innocent abroad. Back home, a dejected-looking Harold reports to a frail Edward. In a world in which regal power was secured by blood, gifts, war and kinship, the king had little left to give. His crown was there for the taking.

The Tapestry moves on to January 1066. Oddly, his funeral is shown before his actual death. Four people are at his deathbed: Queen Edith; Stigand; Robert fitzWimarch, the king's steward; and Harold. The king 'commends his realm to Harold's protection'. Was Harold to be king, or regent for the young prince, Edgar the Aetheling? Whatever the intent, Edward was dead, Harold had the crown and the English nobles (with a few exceptions) rallied to his kingship, since a deathbed wish was considered to overrule any earlier promises. It seemed the Godwins had won, after all.

ABOVE LEFT: *Harold briefs Edward. English bodyguards stand guard behind their masters.*

ABOVE: *Westminster Abbey is blessed by the Hand of God – a symbol of its consecration on 28 December 1065. A workman fixes a weathercock. Within a week, the funeral party, with bellringers, carries the bier of the dead king to the abbey for burial.*

ABOVE: *Edward on his deathbed, with his last visitors (Harold touching his finger, Archbishop Stigand with hand raised, Queen Edith at his feet). The scene shown beneath is of the king's body being prepared for the funeral.*

13

SIGNS AND PORTENTS

ABOVE: *Harold is offered the crown (left) and sits enthroned, with sceptre, orb and sword. Archbishop Stigand stands beside the new king, hardly the stamp of approval in European eyes. Stigand had been Archbishop of Canterbury since 1052, but stood accused of corruption (he owned large estates) and 'pluralism' (he was also Bishop of Winchester). For these reasons, he had been excommunicated by Pope Nicholas II.*

BELOW: *Hunter and hunted. Scenes like this from the Tapestry border often seem to parallel pictures above in the Tapestry, in this case the early scene of William giving orders after Harold is captured by Count Guy.*

Harold's coronation may have been performed by Ealdred, Archbishop of York – a more respectable choice, given Archbishop Stigand's tattered reputation. The Canterbury prelate's appearance in the Tapestry reflects his limpet-like grip on English affairs, and (in Norman eyes) his culpability for Harold's downfall.

As the cheering for King Harold II died away, people commented on a remarkable phenomenon: Halley's Comet, recorded in *The Anglo-Saxon Chronicle* as a 'haired star'. It caused much consternation. *'Isti mirant stella'* (These men wonder at the star) comments the

Bordering on the symbolic

Many of the decorative images in the borders of the Tapestry must have had resonances for people in the 11th century that today are lost. Some hint at allegory. For example, below the images of Harold sailing to Normandy appears this allusion to Aesop's fable of the lion-king and the animals.

Latin text. The comet revisits the Earth every 75 years or so during its marathon tour of the solar system; in 1066 it was particularly bright, being at its brightest in April, though sources suggest it was first sighted in February, not long after Harold's coronation.

In Europe, most people regarded its fiery trail as a sign of God's displeasure and the Tapestry presents a clear juxtaposition: Harold on his throne, the glowing portent in the sky.

The next scene shows a much less composed Harold, listening to a message. From whom? An astrologer, explaining away the comet? A messenger from the North, with news of troubled Northumbria? Or is this an agent, hotfoot from Normandy, bringing alarming reports of William's intentions?

As the king listens, in the scene beneath his feet a flotilla of strange ships drifts. Are these ghostly vessels a portent of invasion?

Next, a small ship beaches in Normandy, a man wading ashore with an anchor. The text says that 'an English ship sails to William's dukedom'. Are these spies hurrying to William? Or English agents, sent by Harold to gather intelligence? War preparations had already begun. The Norman chronicler William of Poitiers, who regarded the comet as a sign of Harold's imminent doom, tells of William sending a captured spy back to Harold with a message. Harold could expect to see his rival 'in the place where he thinks his feet are safest' (i.e. England) within a year – 'or live the rest of his life secure'.

ABOVE: *The appearance of Halley's Comet causes alarm, very probably to Harold as well as his people. The king looks anxious as a messenger brings more bad news. Phantom ships may have figured in his dreams.*

PRELUDE TO INVASION

One significant personality missing from the Tapestry is the home-grown thorn in Harold's flesh, his brother Tostig. Of several Godwin sons, Tostig was probably next to Harold in age, but legend has it that these two brothers were violently opposed to one another, even as boys. King Edward either liked Tostig, or liked mischief-making – giving

LEFT: *A coin minted during Harold's brief reign. It shows one of the few non-Tapestry images of England's last Saxon king.*

BELOW: *'Woodman, woodman spare that tree.' Normans attack the timber with gusto, as shipbuilding proceeds apace. Estimates of the size of William's fleet run as high as 1,000 ships, though many of his vessels must have been small.*

him the earldom of Northumbria, ahead of the rightful heir Waltheof, son of Siward. The disgruntled Northumbrians, being of sturdy and independent mind, rose up against Tostig's harsh rule, and in 1065 the North became a battleground. To restore calm, Tostig was banished to Flanders, to nurse his grievances and blame Harold for again being the 'good' brother.

BELOW: *William soon got wind of Harold's kingship. Messengers and spies crossed the Channel to keep the Duke informed.*

As soon as Harold became king, Tostig started to raid the south and east coasts with a fleet of ships, taking refuge in Scotland when pursued. Rumour whispered that he had offered his services to both William and Sweyn of Denmark, but he finally joined forces with Norway's Harald Hardrada. The Norwegian king is also missing from the Tapestry, but must have been very much in Harold's thoughts as he grappled with the everyday business of kingship in the spring and summer of 1066.

Having formally protested against Harold's accession, William was building alliances in order to gain moral and practical support for a military challenge. The duke is shown in conference with his barons, as he calls in debts and allegiances – requesting ships and men from the local rulers, whom he regarded as his vassals.

As the preparations for war began, life in Normandy took on an urgency beyond that of the seasonal round of providing food and shelter. The Tapestry sequences that cover the invasion planning, and the sea crossing in the late summer of 1066, are among the most fascinating sections of the embroidery.

ABOVE: *Fields still had to be harvested as the summer of 1066 moved on. Scythes, as well as swords, were being sharpened. This illustration from around 1030 shows harvesters at work on English land.*

Winning over the doubters

William in council. His message was that the risks of a sea crossing and battle against a formidable enemy were more than outweighed by the promise of land and wealth. That God was on his side must have played prominently in his advocacy, even if William was not known to be overtly God-fearing.

THE DAILY ROUND

The Tapestry is a rich source of information about daily life in the 11th century, particularly in regard to men's dress and shipbuilding. There are images of homes, humble and grand, and of hunting and farming. Working men's clothes looked much the same as those of their masters, but were made of much plainer coarse fabric. Men wore a tunic-style garment, with tight sleeves and a round neck, long enough to be belted at the waist, hitched up when necessary to keep it dry. When not bare-legged, men wore thigh-length hose or leggings, kept up by fastenings attached to the belt of the braies, a linen undergarment which stopped the wool tunic from being unbearably itchy. The only man in the Tapestry seen to be wearing such a belt is Turold, the dwarf, whose underwear is too big for him. The women (only three are shown in the main body of the Tapestry) wear long dresses.

Glimpses of peacetime labours appear in the border decoration. A ploughman guides a wheeled plough, pulled by a mule or an ass.

RIGHT: *Haymaking; from an Anglo-Saxon calendar. Some of the men work with hand sickles, while others pitchfork the cut hay into a small cart.*

ABOVE: *English peasants prepare the next year's planting. The horse wears a collar-harness, a relatively recent innovation, with shafts or traces attached to what looks like a swingletree on the harrow.*

THIC VENIT:NVNTIVS:AD WIL GELMVM DVCEM

LEFT: *In the lower zone of this section of the Tapestry a huntsman sounds his horn as he unleashes the hounds. Is it coincidence that in the main image above, William is issuing orders – for the ruin of his enemy Harold?*

Another man scatters seed from a bag, and a horse-drawn harrow completes the sowing operation. A bird-scarer drives away hungry crows. In the sections depicting William's camp in England, cooks are shown preparing dinner, and retainers serve the meal to their masters at table. Labourers use picks and spades to build the first Norman fort.

Farming was the mainstay of medieval life. For most people, the daily round left little time for relaxation, but the nobles trained their bodies and horses for war by hunting. William was an avid huntsman and after the Conquest he ordered large tracts of land in England set aside as royal forests. Such forests, like the New Forest in Hampshire, were as much part of the Norman legacy as grim stone castles.

RVM:ET SVI MILITES:EQVITANT: A

ABOVE: *An enthusiastic huntsman, Harold is shown riding out with his hounds and his hawk, in happier times before his trip to Normandy.*

LEFT: *Harvest time: as the summer of 1066 passed, the English farmers brought in their crops while their king watched, and waited.*

INVASION FLEET

The ships of English and Normans are shown in detail, suggesting an artist who knew the sea. The ships are wooden, clinker-built (the planks of the hull overlap), and have oars, a single mast and square sail. The Tapestry's depiction of such vessels is validated by evidence from archaeological finds of Norse ships; for example the Gokstad and Oseberg ships (Norway) and five ships found near Skudelev (Denmark). These typical northern-European vessels were slender and shallow, their prows sometimes decorated with 'dragon' figureheads. A long steering oar was mounted at the stern, and shields hung on the gunwales.

The Normans inherited their skills in shipbuilding from their Viking ancestors, and there were plenty of Normans, Bretons, French and Flemish seamen in William's army experienced in navigating the Channel's choppy waters. The English had seafaring roots too – the Anglo-Saxons who sailed to Roman Britain, and later the Danish Vikings. Ever since King Alfred in the late 800s built

ABOVE: *Workmen cut and shape timber for ships. The man trimming planks (left) wears tunic and hose, although it would have been the height of summer.*

a fleet to fight the Danes, English kings had kept warships ready to defend their coasts.

The Tapestry shows Normans cutting 'green' (unseasoned) timber for shipbuilding. Possibly some of these hastily built ships were expected to be abandoned, or broken up,

after landing. The fresh-cut timber was split into planks, using axes and wedges. Ship-wrights are shown hard at work with axes, adzes and augers. Most of William's ships were probably well-seasoned trading vessels and warships, provided by William's vassals as part of their contribution to the war effort. Showing new ships being built in the Tapestry no doubt emphasized the scale and energy of the Conqueror's purpose.

ABOVE: *One of the Skudelev ships (1070–90), now preserved at Roskilde in Denmark. This was an ocean-going cargo vessel, decked fore and aft, but with an open hold amidships – where horses might be carried. William would have had ships very similar to this.*

LEFT: *In order to launch their ships, men have taken off their hose to wade in shallow water, further evidence that the Norse-style vessels had shallow draughts.*

BELOW: *Axes were weapons as well as tools. This broad-bladed axe head, which dates from the 10th–11th centuries, and is possibly Viking, is similar in design to the battle axes of Harold's housecarls (the king's elite bodyguard). The hardened iron cutting edge is welded on separately. The oval socket would have held a wooden handle, probably of ash.*

READY FOR BATTLE

William planned to ship at least 5,000 men; along with armour, weapons, horses, and wagonloads of other essentials, such as wine. Plenty of ports and estuaries were under his control and therefore at his disposal. Many of his ships were small enough to be hauled up on a beach anyway. From May 1066, vessels began to assemble in the mouth of the River Dives, and as the summer passed, William waited for news from England.

The most encouraging information was that Harold's renegade brother, Tostig, had attacked the Isle of Wight, and then raided the east coast. Later, defeated by Earl Edwin of Mercia, he fled with a dozen ships to Scotland. Tostig may have had some secret contact with William, but the most important result of his raids was that Harold was kept guessing when and where the next attack would come.

By August, the Norman fleet was ready. William's iron will had kept his army together, and fed, without rousing the local population – though few would have risked the Duke's

ABOVE: *Normans carry wine and mail shirts on wooden poles. A cart laden with spears and other war gear trundles towards the beach.*

wrath by protesting. It was a triumph of organization. Unlike William, Harold had problems keeping his levied men in arms – come harvest time, the Wessex men were needed on their farms. By the first week of September, the king had returned to London, and the English fleet in the Channel had dispersed.

William therefore ordered the Norman fleet north, to Saint-Valéry-sur-Somme, just a few hours' sailing from England, only for an adverse wind to hold him up for days.

BELOW: *William's ship,* Mora, *led the way across the Channel, a lantern at its masthead. Horses peer over the gunwales from the ships' holds. Quite how they were unloaded is not made clear in the Tapestry.*

LEFT: *Reconstructed Anglo-Saxon houses at West Stow in Suffolk, and (below) how such houses were shown in the Tapestry. Houses of the time were wooden-framed and often 'boat-shaped', roofed with reed thatch or wooden shingles.*

But even as William fretted, Hardrada made his move, and a fleet of 300 Norwegian ships appeared off the River Tyne. Harold summoned his troops and marched north. The Normans re-boarded their ships, and on 27 September the invasion fleet sailed.

The Tapestry shows the French crossing the Channel at night. Their landing is unopposed. Horses are unloaded, and the Norman cavalry reconnoitres the country-side. There is no fighting, but a rapidly-built wooden fort and the burning of an English house are evidence of Norman intent. William must have expected an attack at any hour, and demanded intelligence from his scouts: where was Harold?

ABOVE: *The Normans dig in, building their first castle in England at 'Hestenga' (Hastings).*

ABOVE: *Pevensey Castle in East Sussex as it can be seen today. The old Roman coastal fortress was taken over and strengthened by the Normans.*

MEN OF WAR

The Tapestry is packed with detail of arms and armour. There are 79 pictured soldiers. Most are Norman knights on horseback or English housecarls on foot. They wear chain mail, and carry shields – most shields are kite-shaped, but oval ones are also shown. Many soldiers wore a body-protector made of fabric or leather, onto which were sewn plates of metal. This was a byrnie. A full coat of linked chain-mail, as worn by a high-ranking knight, was a hauberk. A warrior could wear his sword beneath the hauberk, with the hilt protruding through a slit in the mail. Many common soldiers, like the archers, wore only a leather or padded jerkin, and some of the English appear to be wearing everyday tunics.

ABOVE: *An English seax, a single-edged sword with a slightly curved blade, from which comes the name 'Saxon'. Only 23cm (9in) long, this 10th-century seax is shorter than longswords, which were 75–96cm (30–38in) long and usually two-edged.*

RIGHT: *A mail shirt or hauberk. This German example (1300s), with a later neck collar, weighs 10.4kg (23lbs). It is impossible to work out from the Tapestry what Norman mail was like, but this is close.*

ABOVE: *An army marches on its stomach – and so do noble commanders. Norman cooks prepare dinner for William and his friends, courtesy of English farmers.*

VT CIBVM RAPERENTVR:

HI

Living off the land

The Tapestry shows the Normans foraging for provisions. Horsemen ride out to scout the villages around Pevensey, where the army is camped. Houses are shown at the top of this picture – their occupants having probably fled to safety. Soldiers bring in livestock. A spritely English ox faces the chop. One man carries a pig; another leads a sheep.

Most of the Norman horsemen carry long spears or lances. They could throw, thrust or jab their lances at the enemy. Swords were mostly two-edged long weapons, heavy enough to slice off a head or arm. The horses shown are all male animals. The riders use long stirrups, spurred feet almost touching the ground, which suggests that Norman horses were small (12–15 hands). A massed cavalry charge is unlikely. More probably, William's strategy was threefold: first, archers would rake the enemy lines, firing up into the air, then heavy infantry would close and hack gaps into which horsemen could ride to complete the victory.

The English traditionally fought on foot in the celebrated, but now outmoded, 'shield-wall'. Their most feared soldiers were the elite housecarls, who scythed through the enemy with axes, sword and ash-spears. The Tapestry highlights the heroism of these men, most of whom fought to the death around their king.

RIGHT: *Modern reconstructions of swords, as used at the Battle of Hastings. Surviving medieval swords are usually badly corroded.*

DAY OF DESTINY

ABOVE: *A woman and child flee their home, burned by the invaders.*

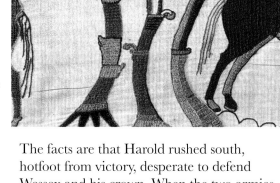

The Tapestry focuses on the Normans, and does not show the two northern battles fought just before William landed. At Gate Fulford near York, an English defeat meant encouragement for Harald Hardrada and Tostig. The second battle, on 25 September at Stamford Bridge in Yorkshire, was a total victory for Harold, the field piled with heaps of enemy dead, among them Hardrada and Tostig.

Three days later the Normans landed. The Tapestry does not show Harold marching south, but he moved fast. Many historians suggest he should have taken his time, rested his men, and called in fresh troops to attack the Normans with overwhelming force.

The facts are that Harold rushed south, hotfoot from victory, desperate to defend Wessex and his crown. When the two armies met, his may have been slightly the smaller.

The Tapestry shows the knight Vital riding to William with news, and an English lookout runs to warn Harold that the enemy is close by. Harold is on horseback (the only English-man shown riding in the Tapestry). On the night of Friday 13 October, the foot-weary English camped on high ground north of Hastings. Next day, at sunrise, the Normans advanced ... and battle began.

LEFT: *Could these scenes be based on eye-witness accounts? To the right, for instance, one Norman soldier is unseated, and slips forward onto the neck of his mount, to slash at an English axeman.*

BELOW: *Massed Normans advance. The border above shows naked figures, one couple seemingly about to embrace: a symbolic commentary? If so, on what?*

ABOVE: 'Here Bishop Odo with staff in hand encourages his boys' *[Latin text].* *Odo rallies the Normans as the English staunchly defend their ground.*

The Tapestry gives a vividly realistic picture of the carnage. Norman knights urge their horses uphill. Spears and arrows fly through the air. English shields are held firm against lance and sword. Archers (shown in the border on the facing page) loose arrows skyward, to fall on the English line. Axes swing; one image shows an English axe slicing into a horse's head. The battle was close-fought. Eustace allegedly urged William to retreat at one point, before himself being wounded and carried from the field. The English might have held their ridge all day, had they not at least twice exposed gaps in their line by pursuing fleeing enemies, thus allowing the Normans to break through.

Accounts of the Battle of Hastings

Possibly the earliest account is the *Carmen de Hastingae Proelio* (Song of the Battle of Hastings), written between 1067 and 1075 by Bishop Guy of Amiens, uncle of Count Eustace of Boulogne. William of Poitiers (Archdeacon of Lisieux 1050–77) wrote an account about seven years after the battle. Odericus Vitalis, born near Shrewsbury about 1075, but Norman through his father, wrote some 70 years later. Another English cleric, Eadmer, wrote his *Historia Novorum in Anglia* (History of Recent Events in England) between 1095 and 1123.

BATTLE WON AND LOST

ABOVE: *Harold's brothers are killed, ridden down by Normans on horseback.*

Horses tumble head-over-heels, axes crunch, arrows hiss, lances pierce armour, flesh and bone. In its battle scenes, the Tapestry shows the Normans as mounted juggernauts, always pressing forward through the marshy lower ground; the English as resolute and terrible in defence of their soil. Shields bristle with arrows – Norman archers kept up a terrible hail of bowshot upon the heads and upper bodies of the close-packed English. Bodies lie broken and maimed in the Tapestry border.

Cries that William was dead spread alarm among the Norman army, and a rout was prevented only by the Duke

LEFT: *The death of Harold. Below in the border, the dead are stripped of their armour and weapons – a familiar epilogue on medieval battlefields everywhere.*

28

Missing bones

The Tapestry gives no clues as to what happened to Harold's body. His Danish mother Gytha offered gold, but William at first refused to hand the corpse over for burial. The mutilated body was later identified by Harold's mistress, Edith Swan-neck. Harold's final resting place is thought to be Waltham Abbey in Essex, but another theory places his bones in a stone coffin at Holy Trinity Church, Bosham.

raising his helmet, to show he was still alive. In such a battle, the death of the leader was often decisive.

Harold had dismounted to fight on foot; his standard flew in the centre of the English position. The turning point of the battle comes with his death, and those of his brothers Gurth and Leofwine (the only other two English names, apart from Harold's, on the Tapestry). The English resistance breaks, and the last scene of the Tapestry shows men running from the field, the Normans in pursuit.

The Tapestry is the first source to record Harold's death by an arrow in the head (by tradition, in the eye). Possibly he was wounded before being cut down: the Tapestry also shows him being felled by a Norman swordsman. According to the *Carmen*

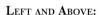

LEFT AND ABOVE:
Medieval arrowheads. William's archers caused heavy losses among the English. Many of Harold's own archers may have been left behind in his dash south.

de Hastingae Proelio, William and three Normans combined to kill Harold – the others being Hugh of Ponthieu (brother of Guy), Robert Giffard, and Eustace of Boulogne. William of Malmesbury (1125) wrote that the English king fell from a bowshot, his brain pierced by an arrow, and was then hacked in the thigh by a Norman sword. Henry of Huntingdon (*c*.1130) described Harold as sinking to the grass beneath a hail of Norman arrows.

ABOVE: *Waltham Abbey, Essex, with, in the foreground, the grave marker and, inset, the stone marking the supposed burial place of Harold II, England's last Saxon king*

AFTERMATH

The Tapestry leaves William in command of a bloodied field. The Conqueror, having been crowned on Christmas Day 1066, set out to subdue his new realm. An attack from Ireland by two illegitimate sons of Harold, and an invasion by Edgar the Aetheling and Sweyn of Denmark were crushed. The burning of York was a fiery symbol of William's ruthless 'harrying of the North', and a chain of castles quickly cowed the conquered. The final flickers of resistance, by Hereward the Wake in East Anglia and by the last English earl, Waltheof, were rapidly extinguished.

In 1070 Stigand was replaced as Archbishop by the reforming Italian, Lanfranc. Odo became Earl of Kent, holding land in 22 English counties and becoming de facto

ABOVE: *An artist's impression of a Norman motte and bailey castle. The motte was a mound, with a stockade on top. The bailey was an enclosure, often ditched or moated, as well as walled.*

co-regent, with William FitzOsbern, Earl of Hereford. Odo set his sights on becoming Pope, and raised a private army to back his candidature. William promptly had him arrested and imprisoned.

ABOVE: *Battle Abbey was built by William on the site of his victory. The dormitory ruins, shown here, overlook the battlefield now walked by thousands of visitors every year.*

The king made four visits to England, sealing his conquest with one of history's great bureaucratic achievements: the Domesday Book of 1086. The following year he died in France from an injury sustained on horseback during yet another campaign. Odo, freed by a deathbed amnesty, schemed against England's new king, William Rufus, and was exiled from England for good.

The Tapestry was hidden, probably shut up in a chest, until it attracted the interest of scholars in the 17th and 18th centuries. The earliest drawings were made at this time by Nicolas-Joseph Foucault, who gave them to the Royal Library in Paris. Another French scholar, Bernard de Montfaucon, had the entire Tapestry drawn in 1730. Antiquarians from England began to visit Bayeux, though the cathedral priests often refused to show their treasure.

During the French Revolution, the Tapestry narrowly escaped being used to cover an army wagon; it was rescued by a lawyer, Léonard Lambert-Leforestier, and other citizens of Bayeux. Napoleon Bonaparte later ordered it to be displayed in Paris, to arouse anti-British sentiment.

ABOVE: *The last, damaged section of the Tapestry. How it ended originally is not known. Perhaps with the coronation of William I, King of England ...*

During the Second World War, the Nazis admired its 'Nordic warrior virtues', and it might have been whisked away to Berlin, but fortunately remained safe first at Sourches (Sarthe) and then in the Louvre, in Paris. Bayeux was the first French town to be liberated by the Allies, and the Tapestry was returned there when the war ended.

ABOVE: *Clifford's Tower in York was just one of many castles built by the Normans to dominate England, at first of wood, later replaced by stone.*

31

LIVING HERITAGE

The Tapestry has been in Bayeux at least since the 15th century, and was probably there earlier. One of Europe's most important historical treasures, the priceless strip of cloth continues to fascinate scholars and visitors, and also provoke keen discussion. Its graphic images evoke admiration for those who made it, those who preserved it and those who fought at Hastings.

Questions remain. Is the Bayeux Tapestry a Norman propaganda exercise, intended to justify William's rights, and therefore the 1066 conquest? Or is it in some ways a more subversive Anglo-Norman creation, made to reconcile former enemies, and more respectful towards Harold than might otherwise have been expected? On balance, it is fair to both sides. No one who goes to see the Tapestry or studies pictures from it can fail to be fascinated, stirred and intrigued by the story it tells.

BELOW: *Mounted 'Normans' recreate the battle at Battle Abbey. The biggest-ever re-enactment in 2006 marked the 940th anniversary of William and Harold's clash at Hastings.*

Places to visit

Ashmolean Museum, Oxford
Battle Abbey, East Sussex – site of the Battle of Hastings
Bayeux, Normandy, France – where the Tapestry is preserved
Bosham, West Sussex: Holy Trinity Church
British Museum, London
Cambridge: Corpus Christi College – has oldest manuscript of *The Anglo-Saxon Chronicle*
Canterbury, Kent: Canterbury Cathedral; St Augustine's Abbey
Dover Castle, Kent
Pevensey Castle, East Sussex
Reading, Berkshire: Museum of Reading – has an 1886 replica of the Tapestry
Royal Armouries, Tower of London and Leeds
Weald and Downland Museum, Singleton, West Sussex
West Stow, Suffolk: Saxon village
Westminster Abbey, London
Winchester, Hampshire: capital of Saxon kings; Winchester Cathedral
York: York Minster; Jorvik Viking Centre; Yorkshire Museum